Diamonds in the Desert

T G Carter

best wishes,

Trevor

WINDMILL HILL PUBLISHING

Diamonds in the Desert

All Rights Reserved

ISBN 978-0-9557426-0-6

First published 2007 by
Windmill Hill Publishing

Printed in Great Britain

To Sally

Contents

Wit and Whimsicality

Love and Lust

Current Concerns

Sense and Sensitivity

Mystery and Mysticism

Wit and Whimsicality

The Adolescent

I no longer want to be alone.
I want to test out my testosterone.
I want to prove how much I've grown.
I want to be a man!

I cannot sleep and cannot rest
Until I find sexual conquest,
And put my urges to the test;
Just to prove I can.

I want approval from my peers,
But don't want them to know my fears,
And the worries of these teenage years.
I want to be accepted.

I want fame and loads of money;
To be intelligent and funny.
Call me 'sir', don't call me 'sonny'.
I want to be respected!

In the mornings I lie late in bed,
Then go to McDonalds to be fed.
It's true that I am easily led,
But I find it all quite pleasant.

You talk to me of misspent youth.
Well; I don't want to hear your truth.
I know I'm vain and quite uncouth,
But I'm an adolescent!

I want fun, not being good.
Bugger doing what I should.
I've got rebellion in my blood
And I want to get it out.

Watch this space for aggravation.
I'll control my situation.
My future will be my creation.
My mind is not in doubt.

I want the beer without the bill.
I want the cure without the pill.
I want it now, and yet still
I don't want to pay.

I want the joy without the sorrow,
And I will beg or steal or borrow.
I can't wait until tomorrow.
I want it all today!

Untitled

I have a domestic issue on which it's hard to get a
grip.
I thought I'd share it with you to perhaps procure a
tip
On what to do about it to arrive at a solution.
So I've summoned up my courage and I've made a
resolution
To share my situation and seek out sympathy.
But it's not for titillation so please treat it seriously.

I have a wonky handle on my bedroom door.
It often comes off in my hand or falls upon the floor.
I've tried to fix it once or twice, but it never holds on
long.
So, whoever fitted this device has clearly got it wrong.

Knobs should always know their place, and stay fixed to their door.
Coming off is a disgrace. It's not what knobs are for!
My wife now finds it very hard to gain access to the room.
She says I am a useless bard who tends to make her fume.

"Why can't you fix this silly knob?": she constantly complains.
I say: "It's not a poet's job". And so the task remains:
Awaiting for a carpenter, a skilful artisan;
Who can study the logistics and devise a cunning plan.

But I've told her if you turn it in a very special way,
And grasp it reassuringly, and don't forget to pray;
Then it often can perform like a normal kind of knob.
It may respond to the affection, and get on with its job.

So until I find an artisan to redeem this situation,
I must struggle on and train my wife in knob manipulation.
And the title of this ditty I have left until the end;
For some may find it vulgar, and I'm hesitating to offend.

But the verse must have its title: of that I cannot rob.
Perhaps, you may have guessed it? Yes. It's called:
"The Naughty Knob".

The Nib-Nob Song

I like nibbling Nib-Nobs
They're naughty and they're nice.
Once you've nibbled on a Nib-Nob
You'll want to nibble twice.
I like nibbling Nib-Nobs.
I nibble them all night.
I nibble them in daylight.
Do you think I am alright?

Nib-Nobs are so knobbly
I'll nibble them for ever.
They make my belly wobbly
But I will never, never
Stop nibbling up my Nib-Nobs;
For I couldn't if I tried.
If I told you that I could
I think I must have lied.

Never nibble your own Nib-Nobs.
It's an anti-social crime.
If you want to nibble Nib-Nobs
Then nibble one of mine.
You can nibble Hob Nobs,
But Nib-Nobs are much better.
So turn a Nob into a Nib
By changing just one letter.

If you can nab a Nib-Nob,
Nab a Nob for me.
Nab at all the Nib-Nobs
Whenever they are free.
Can you nibble up more verses
For this Nib-Nob song?
Imagine you're a Nib-Nob
And it won't take you long.

The Sonnet

It is not hard to write a sonnet.
I'll do it and think nothing of it.
The words provide their own propulsion;
Creating verse by their compulsion.
I've ascertained the formal rules,
And planned how these will all be met.
The rhymes and rhythm are my tools:
The parameters of meter set.
My theme is merely sense of form.
My aspiration to inspire;
Subscribing to an ancient norm,
To elevate it ever higher.
And now I must conclude this sonnet.
Fourteen lines, so now I've done it.

The Old Pig's Sonnet

Each day I struggle on prevailing -
I sail the seas of circumstance.
My efforts seem oft to be failing,
My fate hangs by the thread of chance.
Betumbled is my path with bramble
As I amble onward as I may.
Erstwhile I ran, but now I ramble,
And wish that I were once more gay.
Occluded are the skies above me;
My terra firma less than firm.
I worry no one now could love me,
As worm like on I slowly squirm.
Yet I recall when young and fit
I was content as swine in shit.

Seaside Scenes

Roly-poly are the bowlies that blabber round the
beach.
Bowly-roly waft the wavies as in and out they creach.
Wifty-wafty wends the windies round Roly-poly's
chair.
Oh happy, happy holiday in salty sea breeze air.

The Roly-polies' blubber blobs about the breezy bay.
They slurpy-wurp nice ice cream and harump the
day away.
Seaside slobby wobblies tinkle wrinkling in the sun;
And bulging botties bambling in unselfconscious fun.

What glorious gaddlewandling scintillates the sea
shore's skirt.
What roarious rumpled romplings bumptify all those
who flirt.
Tweedledums do their canoodlings, tweedledees just
twiddle tums,
As dorkleplankton slither in the pondling pads with
chums.

All latch their ecclethruster to its orbit as permits
When charabanking by the seaside and unhinging
happy bits.
Glory be to skallywankling when the season is
fortudinous.
Roly-poly's not conjugled if the resultitude is
ruinous.

Matmata Matters

There's no place less flatter
Than the land round Matmata,
Where the people all still live in caves.
And tourists roll in to examine its matter,
Then roll out again in white waves.

And they tend not to scatter
Too much round Matmata,
But range round the restaurants in groups.
So they leave even fatter than when they got to
Matmata,
And waddle off in satisfied troupes.

Locals gather to natter
In the cafés of Matmata
About the torments of tourist invasion.
They talk of how their traditions will shatter,
Through the incessant European abrasion.

While the touts flaunt and flatter
As they offer knick-knacks that are
All made in China these days.
But the truth of the matter is the tourists aren't
curious
And largely inured to touts' ways.

But it won't greatly matter
What they do in Matmata.
It won't matter to me or to you.
If I stayed here long, I'd go mad as a hatter;
And I suspect that most tourists would too.

(Matmata is a small town in Tunisia where people have
traditionally lived in subterranean houses. It is now heavily
reliant on tourism.)

My Uncle Ed

Uncle Ed has only a head.
He's lacking in bodily form.
He rarely goes out for when getting about
It's hard to keep himself warm.

He has poor circulation and a lack of sensation;
Yet sees and thinks to excess.
His health's only so-so, but his lack of torso
Makes his problems hard to assess.

I've known Uncle Ed since I was a lad.
He's been a great uncle to me.
I've admired his head, though it is rather sad
That that's all Ed seems to be.

But he's great for advice and really quite clever,
At pointing me at the right clue,
Which is very nice, as I hardly ever
Can work out what I should do.

Some say he's inbred and a physical freak,
And really not human at all.
I object to what's said. I think it's a cheek
As Ed thinks ahead of them all.

Love and Lust

Ode to Speed Dating

Love is a fragile flower,
That may devour those who tease it.
And many proffer insights
As to how is best to please it.
Most see mating as a game,
A frame of chains and hidden levers;
Where only fools play by the rules,
And use what tools they can to seize it.
Some jokers offer chances
Of romances by speed dating,
Hoaxing stokers of the glances
Flying furtively to waiting
Hopeful clients now reliant
On this form of tick box gaming
Will accept this form of debt,
And wish to get a chance of baiting
A new connection, a quick inspection,
A swift reflection on offers floating;
By facile smiles, "some other time"s
And all the wiles of scribbled noting;
Around the tables, the secret cables,
The place enables, the egos soaring;
As rapid scoring, hearts out-pouring,
Amidst their fantasies and gloating.
And then the bell spells time to move,
Get in the groove, the next heart rending;
Swift encounter, next disclosure,
Next assessment, next intending;
Of the exposures, false disclosures,
Muddled romp with no sensation;
The clock ticks on, there isn't long
Until the gong signals the ending.

Some will deride this rapid ride,
The quest for bride or chance connection;
Condemn as crude and won't be wooed,
Avoid as lewd and fear infection.
But who's to say, what comes today
Will never stay, and lack duration.
So if it works enjoy the perks,
Ignore the smirks, and risk selection
In chance romance, in verbal dance,
And quick advances of suggestions
To meet again with calmer brain,
When fear is slain by love's digestions.
Then to explore the need for more,
Cut to the core of secret longings;
When need to sin and will to win,
Will have the sting to pierce protections.

A Sunday Love Sonnet

I write a sonnet to my love.
I write to meet her special need.
I seek support from gods above.
I'll ask their help, perhaps I'll plead.
For how can I, in truth, express
Those treasures that her love does bring?
For it's a prize I can't assess.
Perchance that sounds too flattering.
But I think it is too hard by far
To encapsulate by this device.
For I could not map a distant star,
Nor could I sail on seas of ice.
Yet there is this much I can say:
I'm blessed that life's turned out this way.

Ode to a Pink Lady

Moist goodness of your golden globe,
How I wish to lick your lobe.
Firm fruit from fecund fissures formed
Into my willing mouth be warmed,
And masticated with delight;
I'll nibble you all through the night.
With your great goodness I must grapple.
How I want you, luscious apple.

You are the apple of my eye,
Whether raw, or in a pie.
I'll take you, make you one with me,
And I beg you most imploringly -
Submit yourself to my compulsion,
Or I will crumble in convulsion.
You turn my taste buds inside out.
My love for you's beyond all doubt.

Your pinky hues of tender skin
Excite me to prepare for sin.
Your firm white flesh I long to taste
And ravish you in lustful haste.
Oh! I must have you come what may.
I want one like you every day.
Pink ladies line up for my lust.
I'll have you all; I will, I must!

I'll insist I have a daily chomp,
A glorious gastronomic romp.
I can't control my awful urges,
Parts of me are prone to surges.
When it happens I can't hide it,
And so I only try to ride it.
I want you now; to have, to eat;
Without you I'm just incomplete!

I Want a Girl

Prologue

This is a poem without morality
Though it has an immortal theme.
It's preposterous in its elementality
Dripping lust from every seam.

Monologue

I am seeking a female companion,
But my needs are very specific.
Now I'll explain all my requirements,
Which in truth, are rather prolific.

You see, I want a girl who is pretty,
One who is quite beautiful.
One with a really good body,
That other blokes would die to pull.

And I want a girl who is faithful;
One who is not at all risky.
One who can say: 'No thanks mate'
When other blokes get frisky.

She must be well domesticated;
And good at cleaning the sink:
Always dutiful and dedicated,
And concerned with what the neighbours may think.

Also, she must be practical,
And able to knock in a nail;
Animated, but not theatrical;
Hard working, who'll never complain.

She must of course be flexible
And always willing to budge,
And should we have an argument
She'll move on without bearing a grudge.

It's crucial she is kindly;
And always thinks first about me;
With a willingness to follow blindly,
Without questioning how things must be.

But I want a girl who is clever.
One who has been to a college;
Who pursues intellectual endeavour,
Yet respects my superior knowledge.

She must of course be stable:
A sensible chip off the block;
In a crisis strong and able,
As solid and sound as a rock.

But nevertheless she'll be sexy.
And know just how to dress;
Knowing how to present herself
In a way that is bound to impress.

At times she will be kinky
And indulge in experiment,
And be simpering, sexy and slinky,
And enthusiastic in her consent.

And I do like a girl who is funny,
One who can tell a good joke;
One with wit and humour;
Who can laugh at herself, just like a bloke.

My lover must always be passionate;
And seethe with relentless desire;
Yet adapt to life how I fashion it;
And accept she can never retire.

It will help if she is musical,
Perhaps she'll play the guitar
While singing to me as a songbird;
Enchanting, she'll be my star.

But she must also be philosophical,
And able to think in abstractions;
Not limited to just what is topical,
With a wide ranging set of reactions.

Needless to say she'll be cheerful,
I couldn't stand her being depressed.
She must be confident and never fearful;
Especially when supporting my quest.

You see, I want a girl in a million!
One who can meet every need!!
And, I know that she exists somewhere.
I'm sure of it; oh yes indeed!

Anywhere at all

Some like Paris in the springtime.
Others prefer it in the fall.
But I like it with you in November;
In Paris, or anywhere at all.

Current Concerns

Psychopolitics

Putin clings to his gas tap,
And while other leaders see the trap
They're locked into dependency
While claiming to uphold what's free.

As the quagmire of Iraq quakes on,
A vortex of the woebegone
Drawing in more lambs to slaughter,
As no one now tries to report a
Chink of hope amidst disaster.
Everybody knows we're passed a
Point at which mere numbers will
Refloat a civil sense, until
Some kind of reason re-emerges
To transcend the deathly urges
Throbbing in the souls of men
Who care not to return again
To some semblance of civility.
Yet our leaders lack the ability
To admit outright enough's enough;
No, losing face is just too tough.

So bluff and bluster blunder on,
And will do after we are gone.
Some things are just too hard to change,
And no one can defend their range.
It's all entangled and entwining
Us in schemes few are defining
In any way that can make sense,
Except to swathe us in pretence.
As the old cold war has started warming
And we should read it as a warning

Of another fissure opening up
In the global cup from which we sup.
As the edifice looks set to crack,
Increasingly we turn our back,
No longer bothering to pretend
We can control or comprehend.

Suicide Ride

There are no lights at the end of his tunnel,
And all he sees ahead is a fatal funnel.
The only lights he sees are the searchlights in his
eyes.
The boy's in trouble. He's on a suicide ride.

Whatever you do it won't be good enough.
Whatever sanctions you try he'll treat as mere bluff.
Those offering him escape he despises as spies.
The kid can't be reached. He's on a suicide ride.

It's said by romantics that childhood should be
magic,
But this boy's days are distorted, sad and tragic.
Everyone who tries to help, he will cruelly deride.
This boy is not listening. He's on a suicide ride.

His head is dead, his soul is lost, his spirit is
tormented.
The only world he sees is one he has invented.
Friends are not his style, and anger is his bride.
This kid's a real case. He's on a suicide ride.

There's venom in his words, and poison on his
breath.
The only games he wants to play are those designing
death.
The real world and this boy are unlikely to collide.
His time is running out. He's on a suicide ride.

Games are not for play, for he must always win.
You won't find compassion inside this young skin.
It may not be long now until the life blood's dried.
For this kid is not for turning. He's on a suicide ride.

Is this story true or just wild exaggeration?
Is the boy emblematic of our youth's alienation?
But how do we reach him, what shall we do?
Should we step aside? He's on a suicide ride.

Johannesburg

Behold the high walled city, as prolifically it sprawls.
There's more scorn than love or pity seething safe
behind its walls.
It's a ghost town megatropolis as soon as dusk
descends,
Though by day its febrile factions do their best to
make amends.

For the history that's no mystery is a burden to
despise
As divisions can't be hidden, and they've no time to
analyse
The schisms in the rhythms that pulsate in the
desire
To wheel and deal and steal their way inside the
concrete pyre.

And from the crannies of the continent dispossessed disciples come
To carve into its edifice their own stake in its sum.
And there's hunger in their bellies, and there's pain in every heart;
But their heads are full of dreams of schemes of making a new start.

And the city draws them like a magnet at a thousand souls a day,
And imbues them with its energy as they strive to make their way
In its cauldron of comeuppance where illusions are shattered;
Where they put distance from their past and the things that once mattered.

But identity and destiny are no longer aligned,
As the new order's borders are only roughly defined.
So the fast lanes beckon to those with the bottle
As the city speeds towards tomorrow with an open throttle.

And the equation cannot balance, for there's always new additions;
More zeros on the sum, still fighting for positions;
And the going gets tougher, and the winners more defended.
Johannesburg: the city of civility surrendered.

Stranger Danger: Adolescent Concerns

You preach of stranger danger,
You urge me to "take care".
You magnify the danger,
Saying: "It's not safe out there".

You teach me to be wary.
You tell me not to trust.
You say: "The world is scary".
You insist to me I must:

Never talk to strangers.
Never stay out late.
Beware of all life's dangers.
Be careful who I date.

Be mindful who I talk to.
Be modest what I show.
And also that I ought to
Make plans before I go.

Well, I respect your good intentions,
But I'm finding it too much.
Now I think I need to mention
That I'm feeling out of touch.

You see, I need to be a ranger.
I need to take some chances.
I want to dice with danger.
I'm ready for romances.

So lay off this "stranger danger".
There's a danger I can't breath.
I need some space to range or
Very soon I'm gonna leave.

The Acephalic Nation

Behold the headless nation;
How heedlessly it acts.
Its bureaucratic congregation
Confused by tick box tracts.

Behold its legislation;
Its edicts of quick fix,
Its facile exclamation,
Its battered bag of tricks,

Its push-me-pull-you policy,
Its tabulations of deceit,
Its pretensions and pomposity
That won't concede defeat.

It's minced our education.
It's heated up our air.
It's fomented mass frustration.
It's led us to despair.

It's an acephalic monster
And I fear how it reacts,
And yet we're forced to sponsor
Its actions through our tax.

I fear I have no answers.
I feel it's quite a mess.
I think we've missed our chances.
I sense it's causing stress.

(acephalic: headless)

Internet

Colossus of communication,
Your tendrils spread into each nation,
Controller of imagination,
Oh great god Internet;
Oh bringer of the winds of change,
Through you we can always engage,
No subject is beyond your range
From New York to Tibet.

Give us each day broadband connection,
Dictate to us our next direction,
Subject our souls to your inspection,
And bestow identity;
Your wondrous web extends world wide,
Now there's nowhere left to hide,
We all kow-tow and have complied
With how we need to be.

In distant days of pen and ink
When we had books and time to think,
Before we knew that magic link
To modern information;
Before we knew we could afford it,
And just how well the world rewards it,
For logging on into your orbit
Of media domination.

Great was the time that we did waste,
Tough were the tests that we once faced,
But now we know that 'cut and paste'
Is all we have to do
To get a good two-one degree
From a modern university,
And overcome adversity
By clicking right on cue.

The Race

All the races fight for spaces on this ever shrinking
earth,
As the pace of competition gathers heat.
And they face the fearsome future claiming to uphold
its worth,
But their impulse is always to compete.

And this erases all the traces of the noble
sentiments,
And so defaces those statements of intention;
The ideals of which splinter when they meet
impediments,
So calls to act fizzle out into abstention.

We can't control pollution and hence there's no
solution;
But place your bets, life's still a bagatelle.
For as the guilt is all collective there's no point in
persecution:
We're all just victims of the glamour of the spell.

So it seems there are no aces that can cap the trap
we've made,
As the point of no return goes flashing by.
So if destiny looms unaffected by whatever cards are
played,
Then maybe there are no more tricks to try.

Now it's knowledge commonplace that we've flunked
this steeplechase,
And we can't regenerate our spent forces.
And so we face the final feature of our human
history's race:
A desperate dredge for diminishing resources.

Sense and Sensitivity

An Exposition on Sins of Omission

We all commit sins of omission
By all the kindnesses left undone.
I think it's a fair proposition
As others oft pay for our fun.

It's hard to say with informed precision
How those undone acts can deform us,
But I think it's a fair proposition that
The accumulated effects are enormous.

And although it can be a tricky decision
To distinguish our need from our greed,
I think it's a fair proposition
To take care where we scatter our seed.

For if it thrives without supervision,
The result could be heartache and pain,
So I think it's a fair proposition
To be mindful which seeds turn to grain.

And we all commit sins of omission
By excesses of circumspection.
So is it not a fair proposition that
Honest men should not fear inspection?

Should our accounts not be free of revision,
And not fearful of scrutinisations?
And is it not a fair proposition
To apply this to all organisations?

Yes, we know life is rife with division,
And we identify most with our own,
But I think it's a fair proposition
That our patterns are not cast in stone.

No, we need not entrench that position.
We could challenge the rules of the game.
For if no one heeds this proposition
It's likely to stay much the same.

Yes, sad are the sins of omission
When we avert our eyes from the fray.
I think it's an unreal proposition
That we don't all do this every day.

So you'll agree now with my supposition
That we all think too much of ourselves,
And you'll support now this fair proposition
That we don't leave those good deeds to the elves.

Don't dismiss this plea with derision.
Our futures all hang on your plans!
I know this is a tall proposition,
But we all must adjust our demands.

For we are drifting towards a collision.
As a species we're losing our touch.
Still I think you've heard this proposition,
So I won't repeat it too much.

I hope you've liked this exposition,
And think of how you can make a new start.
And I'll conclude with a fine proposition:
That we take its entreaties to heart.

Ode to Communication

Words are not always exact.
Do not accept them as a fact.
Do not assume an instant meaning.
Subject them to a lengthy screening.
(Except when you are in a hurry
Then check the Oxford Dictionary.)
And though it may provoke abuse,
Defend good words from wild misuse.

For language is a precious gift:
Abuse should cause you to be miffed.
Though the effort spent may seem absurd,
Consider how you use each word,
For semantics is a crucial game,
And meanings aren't always the same.
You too can dissect and dissemble
To see what meanings may resemble.

But don't delight in dour pedantic
Snipes at styles from North Atlantic
American English deviations;
You should respect their variations.
For it's indigenous illiteracy
That limits how our life can be.
So why not start a revolution
To promote literacy and elocution.

Be a fanatic and become obsessed!
Put every utterance to the test.
Scrutinise the connotations
And explore the many variations.
For there would be less indecision
If words were used with more precision.
I hope this plea is not too late.
Please go forth and communicate!

A Rumination on Motivation

We all follow our paths from perceptions
In the light of our own situation.
Yet the world is rich in deceptions
And clouded by misinformation.
We search for sense and satisfaction
To make life's journey worthwhile.
We respond to all kinds of attraction
To cultivate our own lifestyle.

We count our wealth by measuring tangibles
And the accounts held in our bank.
Yet when we try to locate the imaginables
Our imagination can often go blank.
So we count all the things that are countable
And ignore all the things that matter.
We set sights on the clearly surmountable
And work around all those things that are......

Hard to describe, and yet elemental
To the central requisites of life:
Things elusive, but clearly essential
To divest us of spiritual strife.
Can you sense that sense that I speak of?
Are we not more than the sum of our parts?
Is it the quest that philosophers reek of:
To explore things we can't map on charts?

So it's the processes more than the product
That we should be focused upon:
And the norms and forms of our conduct
That can carry us forward as one.
(I hope you like this rumination
And cogitate on how it connects
To your socio-personal situation
And the emotions that it infects.)

Freedom (a Philosophical View of)

Can a bird be free from the skyways?
Can a politician be free from election?
Can cars be free from the highways?
Can a penis be free from erection?
Yet your ways may not be my ways -
We're subject to different proclivities.
Though some advocate do or die ways
To overcome life's instabilities.

A space can't be free from dimension.
A poem can't be free from a rhyme.
(Though some poets reject this contention,
It applies to all poems of mine.)
A ticket can't be free from inspection.
A sail can't be free from its mast.
A writer can't be free from reflection.
Our future can't be free from our past.

Though it's true that we are given choices,
We are moulded from our conception.
We're controlled by subconscious voices
That dictate how we make a selection.
We are driven by lust and biology
To do the strange things that we do.
So 'freedom' is just a mythology;
An abstraction that's clearly untrue.

And I expect you'll detect more examples
From the ample connections I've given.
For my listings are merely some samples
Of how life is connectively driven.
Nobody is free from connection
From the day of their birth to their death.
One thing always joins to another.
We're dependent on air for each breath!

Calendric Notches

Calendric notches aggregate
Until we find our final date;
Succumb at last to worldly fate
And end our conscious story.
We mark the years and ages passing,
But not the wealth of knowledge massing,
Or the borrowed time we are trespassing
On in search for glory.

As time entombs us yet enables
Each to fashion flags and labels;
To set aside the myths and fables
And define our space and time.
And cover crimes of careless actions
With excuses built on vague abstractions,
Justified by selfish satisfactions
To inflate our sense of prime.

While media monsters once created
Gnaw at our core with teeth serrated.
Yet bleeding, bruised and enervated;
Some still reject the lie.
And cry alone, but joke with peers;
And stagger on through joy and tears,
And fight the nights of haunted fears
Until it's time to die.

The Sense of Sages

Through all the ages there have been sages who sort
our fact from fiction.
And for their wages they write pages and offer wise
prediction.
Every age has had its sages to codify its special sense
Of how that age is to engage with its own intelligence.

Priests of the past, of regal caste who disseminated
fear;
So righteously they cast their vast empires of austere
Sets of rules for feeble fools to entrap their minds
In tight capsules, in high walled schools that time
has left behind.

Now we encounter different binds with undefined
'celebrities',
Who broadcast bunk into the minds of minions with
ease.
So crisis looms; confusion rules, and response is in
convulsion;
With sages now replaced by fools whose god is mere
consumption.

I Write

I write to you to enlighten;
Not to deter, to depress or to frighten,
Or to cause your nerves to tighten.
No; I write to you to enlighten.
Some poets write to encumber
You with woes too many to number.
Their worries will haunt you in slumber,
When their verses encase and encumber.

I like words that convey a conviction,
Which don't wallow in dereliction;
I know it's hard to make a prediction,
But at least we should offer conviction.
Some poets will wallow in sorrow,
Pronouncing no hope for tomorrow.
Well, I've a notion that they can borrow,
Sorrow's not for wallowing in.

I like poems of perspicacity
That display thought, and wit and audacity:
That promote fine writing's capacity
To enrich our thinking by their sagacity.
I like meanings to be ascertainable
In a style that's quite entertainable;
But some poems are not penetratable,
So their worthiness must be debatable.

Still, I'll do my best to enlighten;
To delight and deliberately brighten.
I'm writing, I'm writing, I'm writing
To enlighten our future; okay.

Dealing with Feelings

I can deal with feelings.
I'm a sensitive sort of person.
As anyone will tell you,
I'll never have an aversion

To taking on others problems
And then talking them through.
I will never be judgemental
When a friend is feeling blue.

I can always keep a secret.
I am the soul of discretion.
And everyone feels better
After making a confession.

Getting things off your chest
Is a part of the solution.
Just let it all come out;
Expel emotional pollution.

I am good with feelings.
I listen actively for hours:
I reframe the problems;
I find that it empowers.

We make a cup of tea
Then sit down at the table.
I will offer sympathy
As far as I am able.

Everyone has feelings;
Except of course myself.
When I feel a feeling coming on
I just shove it on a shelf.

The Counselling Poem

Are you falling into pieces, but can't entirely fall
apart?
Do you need a new beginning, but don't quite know
where to start?
Do you need help to answer questions, but don't
quite know who to ask?
Are the cogs of your conscious being daunted by life's
tortured tasks?

Is your life-spark under heated, has your sparkle
ceased to shine?
Are your demons dancing undefeated, is your drive in
dire decline?
Is your carburettor clogged up, is your engine out of
oil?
When you're faced with a new challenge, is your
response just to recoil?

Is your motivation mangled by the tracks that you
have trod?
Do your thoughts feel torn and tangled, ravelled up
and rather odd?
Has your will to win been jaded by always being
second best?
Is your body now abraded, and all worn out by
nature's tests?

If to all these searching questions, you concede a
yawning - yes:
It's safe to say you have a problem that sometime
soon you should address.
You may need a change of partner, change of job or
change of place.
You may need to see a doctor, or seek out a tranquil
space.

Better not to be a martyr on a path you can't sustain.
Read again 'Desiderata', it may help to soothe your pain.
Review your heartfelt aspirations; what can make you feel content?
Identify your inspirations; redemption won't be heaven sent.

Make a list of all your assets: what are those you need to add?
When you've considered all your facets, life may not seem all that bad.
Transcend yourself from this position; release yourself from feeling blue.
Renew your soul by self cognition. For answers must begin with you.

I Believe

I believe that it all will come right in the end:
I believe that the barriers will buckle and bend;
That right will be mighty and someday will send
The conditions of my satisfaction.
I believe to receive that you first have to send;
And invest your conviction in what you intend;
And to try to be true, but not to offend
When transmitting a thought to an action.

I believe that agendas are often unclear;
And that love often struggles to overcome fear;
As we wish on the stars but cling to what's near
As part of our human condition.
I believe we need challenge to be satisfied;
That life wasn't designed as a sweet easy ride;
That aversion to risk is failure's bride
And results in retarded ambition.

And I believe in ambition as spiritual fuel;
Although cynics will sneer and think it's uncool;
But he who laughs last is rarely a fool
For he indicates his power.
And even those minions entered as pawns;
As the first to fall when the conflict dawns;
May transmute themselves to higher forms
If they can choose their hour.

I believe that there's lots out there to be had;
And there's probably more of the good than the bad;
And that you don't need to be a Sir Galahad
To seize your situation.
So I believe that life is worth thinking about,
Though its rights and wrongs ever generate doubt;
It's better by far to be inside than out
And worth the rumination.

Mystery and Mysticism

Ode to the Desert

The desert sands are formless, and submit to no
demand,
And their ever changing patterns, mock the things
that we have planned.

Now I'm escaping to the desert, and I'm hoping there
to find
Some peace and quiet essence in a place I can
unwind.
And I'm hoping that the desert keeps the city's strife
at bay;
And the power of the desert will have truth it won't
betray.

For the desert sands are formless, and submit to no
demand,
And their ever changing patterns mock the things
that we have planned.

Man seeks to strive and conquer in the irrigated
lands;
But disdains the cultivation of the seas of desert
sands.
On the oceans, in the mountains, still he strives to
subjugate;
Yet the desert he abandons to the fickle sands of fate.

For the desert sands are formless, and submit to no
demand,
And their ever changing patterns mock the things
that he has planned.

And the desert casts a pattern that human history emulates,
As from dust to dust it stumbles unaware of future fate.
For there's no shade in the desert from the unoccluded sun,
And its power unimpeded will divide the human sum.

For the desert sands are formless, and submit to no demand,
And their ever changing patterns mock the things that we have planned.

In awe of its dominion man tries to map its ways;
But the desert is undaunted, it advances and it strays,
Encouraged by man's habit to pollute his canopy
Of protection from the power of the sun's insistency.

Yet the desert sands are formless, and submit to no demand,
And their ever changing patterns mock the things that we have planned.

Unresisting, and persisting with his need for cheaper travel,
Man causes the protection of his future to unravel.
In his need to get away from his nest of corporate scrabble,
His inheritance he'll pay through his reckless need to dabble.

Still the desert sands are formless, and submit to no demand,
As their ever changing patterns mock the things that we have planned.

In the tamed and temperate regions man dictates
and man advances;
Man constrains and man constructs; but still the
desert dances,
As it shimmers round the cities like white icing on a
cake,
As it glimmers on those passing, casting shadows in
their wake.

As the desert sands are formless, and submit to no
demand,
And their ever changing patterns mock the things
that we have planned.

And those who idolise the city with their idiot empty
eyes,
Who look with scorn and pity, who hide behind the
lies
Of the grasping urban warriors who seek to terrorise
And misdirect their energy to seek a worthless prize;

Will find the sands are formless, and ignore their
vain demand,
As the ever changing patterns mock the things that
they have planned.

For the desert holds a mirror to the vacuum of their
goal;
Through the cloud of the distortion to the dust bowl
of their soul:
And all misplaced ambition based on pecuniary
success,
It dismisses with derision, exposing its excess.

And still the sands are formless, and submit to no demand,
As their ever changing patterns mock the things that they have planned.

For the desert has integrity, it seeks not to disguise;
Its extremes are all external, it won't need to dramatise
Its power, and its purpose for the age that we are in.
The desert holds its virtue as the city steeps in sin.

For the desert sands are formless, and submit to no demand,
And their ever changing patterns mock the things that we have planned.

Yet the desert won't desert you unless you desert yourself.
For the free and open-hearted it will elevate their health:
By the expanse of its being, by its purity of air;
By its order of disorder you can find your spirit there.

For the desert sands are formless, and submit to no demand,
And their ever changing patterns mock the things we all have planned.

For the desert's not deserted, but its riches held in trust;
And they wait to be alerted by those who can adjust
To the aspects of its wonder, and the challenge it presents
To cast your soul asunder from modernity's torments.

For though those sands are formless, and submit to
no demand,
Their simplicity informs us and may help us
understand.

For the aged it is refuge, perspicacious to the youth;
For each can find a message emanating from its
truth.
The desert holds its answers for those who do
inquire;
For those submitting presence to the soul of its
empire.

Though the desert sands are formless, they may
sense that wild demand:
As their ever changing patterns mock the things we
all have planned.

An Ode to Memory

I don't know what it is with the memory,
But sometimes it won't let you forget
Things that you don't want to remember,
Things that, perhaps, you regret.

On the other hand, it can be remarkable
When you see into the future and get
Glimpses of what hasn't happened,
About things that have not occurred yet.

I think it plays tricks to confuse me.
Because sometimes when I like it least,
It haunts and taunts to abuse me
Like an unwelcome ethereal beast.

Yes, a very strange thing is the memory;
It seems like it's a mind of its own.
And whether as a friend or an enemy,
It emerges when I am alone.

It sometimes looms out from the darkness
And presents things in fathomless visions,
That can disturb by the style of their starkness,
And refute my attempts at revisions.

Yet, when I call for its help, it's selective.
Its information is riddled with gaps.
It's a better gossip than a detective.
Its concentration can easily lapse.

Now, if we could understand all that we remember
Whilst still in the spring of our life,
Without waiting for our final December
To dismember the torment and strife;

Would we all become wise and enlightened
And adjust our beliefs and our aims?
Would we feel confident, free and entitled
To see beyond our cultural frames?

Some people think that we have a forgetory
Where sad memories can go to be minced.
And while I earnestly wish that there'd better be;
To be honest, I'm not really convinced.

Still, that could be a useful illusion,
As I should end on a comforting note.
So, despite all its grief and confusion
My memory can still have my vote.

For when all's said, I wouldn't be without it.
And I think that we never will part.
And although often enough I will doubt it,
I still feel it's in touch with my heart.

And there's an aspect of its resemblance
That seems well established and set.
It's the gift of a special remembrance:
That is, that you and I've met.

Intransigence

There's always some kind of reason for standing
where we are;
And a silver spoon is feeding some beneath their
lucky star,
While the outsiders are baying to the moon forlorn
and far:
Lacking courage to feel aspiration.
There's always been a kind of logic to determine what
we do;
And as the stars smile and sparkle and enjoy what
they accrue,
The dogs in their black holes will puzzle at their view;
As alter egos sigh in resignation.

There's always been a scheme of things that's rather
hard to change;
That the cowboys can ride hard and fast and
dominate their range;
While the shepherds shudder in the wind, and fail to
quite engage;
As the sheriff tries to stifle his laughter.
Yet there's always been a notion that it isn't all quite
right;
That echoes round the universe in the dead of night,
And calls to the dispossessed "it could be time to
fight,
And if not, you'll be damned for ever after".

But there will always be a reason why the call is
never heard;
And there will always be a fearfulness to blank out
every word;
And there will always be an instinct to dismiss it as
absurd,
And stay, safe and cold, in their station.

Dear Comrade

Ghosts of the past that last, that linger,
Claw at your mind with withered finger,
Cling on to thoughts that cause distortions.
Don't look back, dear comrade.
Had we used a different road map
We'd have only found a different head trap;
Wrapped ourselves in other cautions.
Don't look back, dear comrade.

The shadows shrink as we make distance,
They won't persist with their resistance;
They're just the dust of echoes fading.
Don't look back, dear comrade.
Death will take us soon enough.
Before it does, it likes to bluff;
Reminding as it's always raiding:
Take your chances, comrade.

Dance with ghosts and they'll erode you.
Cut them down so they can't hold you.
Be bold and cold with old encumbrance.
You don't need it, comrade.
Sleep now to prepare for morning.
The ghosts cannot postpone its calling.
Leave them to their own remembrance.
Don't look back, dear comrade.